Ecce Homo and Nine Painters

Also by Adrian Rogers and published by Ginninderra Press
The Sun Behind the Sun
Between Two Hemispheres
The Prisoner's Messenger
The Medicine Wheel
Music is a River of Life
A Way Less Travelled
Seasons, Situations and Symbols (Pocket Poets)
Flowers and Star Signs (Pocket Poets)
Human Nature & the Welfare State (Pocket Polemics)
Croagh Patrick (Pocket Places)
Port Victoria (Pocket Places)

Adrian Rogers

Ecce Homo
and Nine Painters

To a Golden Leo, in the Light

Ecce Homo and Nine Painters
ISBN 978 1 76109 111 7
Copyright © text Adrian Rogers 2021
Cover image: Robert Lederer on Unsplash

First published 2021 by
Ginninderra Press
PO Box 3461 Port Adelaide 5015 Australia
www.ginninderrapress.com.au

Contents

Botticelli
- Venus — 9
- Nocturne 1 – Winter — 10
- Virgin — 11
- Savonarola — 12
- Ecce Homo 1 – Destiny — 13

El Greco
- Agony in the Garden — 17
- Nocturne 2 – Night Creatures — 18
- Cleansing the Temple — 19
- Cracked Ice — 20
- Ecce Homo 2 – The Unanswered Question — 21

Michelangelo
- Creation — 25
- Nocturne 3 – Bells — 26
- The Universal Myth — 27
- Fasting in the Dark — 28
- Ecce Homo 3 – Eyes on the Back — 29

Rembrandt
- Emmaus — 33
- Nocturne 4 – Moon Past Midnight — 34
- Self-portrait — 36
- Raindrop World — 37
- Ecce Homo 4 – Eyes on the Eternal — 38

Constable
- The Water Mill — 41
- Nocturne 5 – Hunted — 42
- Cathedral in the Rain — 43

A Strong Light	44
Ecce Homo 5 – The Scourge	45

Turner

Sunset From a Train	49
Nocturne 6 – Dark Visions	50
Castle Loom in Dawn Light	51
Lord of the Sun	52
Ecce Homo 6 – The Image	53

Van Gogh

Sunflower King	57
Nocturne 7 – The Morning Star	58
Dancing in the Corn	60
Does the Iris Remember?	61
Ecce Homo 7 – Those Eyes	62

Sydney Nolan

Ned Kelly – First-class Marksman	65
Night Watch	66
Ned Kelly – The Trial	67
Love – In Light and Shadow	68
Ecce Homo 8 – At the Crossroads	69

Nicholas Roerich

Altai Dreaming	73
Dare to Dream	74
Messenger of the White Burkhan	75
Road to the Seventh Gate	76

Botticelli

Venus

Sun-gilded cream glowing
foam-flaunting flourishing
across aquamarine
conceals, through steep
and shallow-sided waves
secrets shaded, depth
dark yet rising into light
lustrous, blue/green
for Venus, a sheen
dazzling the shell-born
dancing riotously sea/wild,
kaleidoscopically colouring
memories,
flowering in moments
accepted yet upended
by glitter-gold sea-born
fantasias painting light,
outlining beauty
dreaming envisioned duty
dying by sun, shade and
aqua-blue catching violet
above the horizon.

Nocturne 1 – Winter

Evening has bite and beauty
grey frost
half light
a thin clarity of air
a distantly wounded sunset
red/cold and still.

Voices harrowed by duty
sounding lost
echo white
and cold, trees share
a still unwillingness to let
time move and fill

this winter day's slow dying
to capture
homing birds flying
into bare branched trees,
a dark rapture
into moonrise, the lees
of memory growing.

Virgin

Our painter has her limned
white/gold/green over blue
starred, crowned in spring's
florescence.

True Isis, innocently knowing
first a white robe
then barefoot goes to black
her gown gold untrimmed.

Stars, as above so below
daringly showing
their commerce with angels
are growing in wisdom
disproving sceptics
in holy desiring.

Imagine a forget-me-not virgin
mother
crone untimed, firing
for lives unrhymed, loving
in tandem with higher selves,
rainbow graces,
delving into our spaces.

Savonarola

A wind off the river chilled foul
exudes a miasma of death
a day/night offence cloud covered
heavy and dank, no respecter
of persons or rank.

Conscience averse looks away
as penitence processional
mark of hope recessional,
visible breath insubstantial
yet by signification stark
is feebly lank as a river flow's
heedlessness
like a street stalking plague infecting
aspiration and selfishness.

Innocence 'passes by', astray,
a clock chimes the hour yet to be.

A city of art, colour, glitter-spiking lust,
crimes, liking, unliking Dante's ghost
excoriating licence, fails to see One
speaking truth to power.

'Behold the Man!'

Ecce Homo 1 – Destiny

Ecce Homo, not
moonlight on marble or
water flow,
just destiny…

whose lot is hoar
with time-bound frost
cast and crowned where go
passers-by averting selves
from testifying stone, a vast
emptiness where delves
disinterested
one fulfilling the self
prophetically invested,
Gethsemane-sheltered
beneath its olive trees
enduring
like iron tested.

El Greco

Agony in the Garden

Eyes, for many febrile paces
cross-stitching the scene from end to end
confronting
an evening, as in Spain often is
springing not so different
from another time and placing
a Passover evening melding into night
confronting
a glance inescapable facing
all possible futures, attending
a painter with little to gain
yet vision to bring
influences confluent with inner sight,
confronting
the Angel of the Agony, passers-by
their haunted selves away-turning
confronting
those eyes reluctantly as though to justify
unwillingness, acknowledging
a crossing over to revelation's inner-lit
tranced stillness and a grove of olive trees
confronting
the agony, the love, the everlasting light.

Nocturne 2 – Night Creatures

A breath of darkness
velvet soft unto death
underfoot, tree-housed
aerial acrobatic
rustles leaves,
pounce, snap,
but no one grieves
when no prismatic cast
of moonlight touched
by other than breath
accompanies
on their homeward way
those small things
darkly undefined by hope
when moonlight's
watery silver lope
approaches
spring, summer
and the leaf fall mantra
not protected when Death's
chanting light's remnants
correctly slanting
overshadowed are…

Cleansing the Temple

On a day sky-clear average
for spring
along the road to Passover
a surrounding
city-riotous clamour disturbs
the trading moments, curbs
hopes for peace
through wrung-out hours
and a material flood powers
across paved Temple courts
for the profitable chink
of hard driven rorts.

Let it be, beyond reason
in and out of season
unresolved, unbound
until sandalled feet hardened
by stone-roughened roads
set straight a course unburdened
by bantering trades
angered at desecration
in a sacred space
for grace deferred while
His whip, scourging
the profit motive, restoring
a house of prayer
defies time's race, purging
the universal soul for love.

Cracked Ice

A smoothly pallid grey
light tricked surface
cracks across
before slipping away

like the Lay
of the Last Minstrel
leaving time
an emasculating transience
of temporary magic
whose moment is
inevitability scarred,
seeming a permanently
illusory
lake or river iced
into temporary stillness
time the enemy, giver
of tricking un-timeliness,
a seasonal shard
of un-mindfulness.

Ecce Homo 2 – The Unanswered Question

Not Botticelli's dreaming
nor Master Veronese
and the Church's scheming,
I cannot seize
impassioned a Sistine creation
of Adamic yet Divine dictation.

Beyond incantation I, soundless
am a face
the unanswered question
grace
love boundless
leaving
unavoidably, an implication…

from grieving
my numinous haunted eyes
cannot release you
but be true
to what never dies, love.

Michelangelo

Creation

I am flat-backed, racked,
a crucifying scaffolding
my upholding
freed only in spirit
for ceiling wet plaster uncracked
and brush strokes unfolding,
melding
spread-wide a legacy
beyond the traditional,
eye, arm, and hand Adam
calling into being
eyes widely innocent, facing
the Godhead
flaring red, orange, yellowed
hinting flesh tones consonantal
green, blue, indigo, fed
in a cosmos crowned violet,
a mellowed splendour of maturity
for Cardinals gazing
eyes inset on colours,
only seeing
while I, beyond being
have caught the eternal light.

Nocturne 3 – Bells

Bell calls ice dark
claw the night
echo-roll-resonating
wind-gust-cut,
booming into the backfall.

At winter's gate
fire is a lesser spark
than the toll
of a passing bell
disseminating
less than a strut optimising
fate's earth-slow passing.

Retreat…!
Sound the Last Post
across a moon-path
coast to coast, delete
frittering memories glittering
backwashed into history
night's looming
self-scheming presence
slouching towards dawn
presaging hope's gleam
echoes, shadowing.

The Universal Myth

Leaping from printed page
painted canvas sculpted stone
Alma, divine Parthenos
mystery universal, history
myth, all seasons a virgin
for veiled reasons
by the Nile searching
for brokenness amid reeds

or from sleeping seeds
on clear hard winter nights
birthing the Winter King
when for Mithras in his cave
the angels sing
while shepherds guard
futures yet to be.

Her offspring see
long ages in the tree of life's
ten stages, one hidden
and, when spring ranges
in the eternal cycle's
sun flashed waters
flowers, grass and trees
the Universal Virgin
rings time's changes.

Fasting in the Dark

Sap flowing from a cut tree
in small hours dark
is blood from the heart
until day breaks night's spell.

'Let there be light.'

Love anchors us, and we
enduring who mark
Lent's fast in that part
of the soul's broken shell
so austere
in pain and some fear
with ash on the soul
await our releasing
when the bells toll
fears ceasing
as day becomes bright,

'till then…
don't let the sun go down.'

Ecce Homo 3 – Eyes on the Back

Conscience is a rack
whereon I, stretched,
frozen, not meeting
eyes on my back…wait
to be greeted?

Ecce Homo…the image
arrested
heart, soul, doom, goal
invested is, for what?

Death, be no cul-de-sac
but a lot cast
confronting those eyes
for one on track
to win the prize…eternity.

Rembrandt

Emmaus

Sandals no protection were
against hard roads grit-rough,
the foot-stirred dusted
ever lengthening walk
of disillusioning
severing the connection
of rusted passing years
covering friendship's memories
locked away,
until a fellow traveller
companionably in passing
linked the Far World
through its portal
with the sun/sky near world
of today
at tired day's end when mortal
natural hospitality
guested a stranger
in lamp-lit evening at the table
breaking bread,
scarred hands telling in story
the pain…
and the glory.

Nocturne 4 – Moon Past Midnight

Moon/gold/pale enigmatic
in bloodless beauty
betrays Rusalka
and lovers everywhere
none hiding anywhere
from etiolated scrutiny
with chanted intensity

a listless hymn
a shimmer/floating path
across star/struck water
somewhere,
piercing a nowhere
thin-fingered
forest swaying canopy
windless, wordlessly,
or drenching sand,
stone, and sinless black
abiding rock surfaces

guiding interfaces,
questing Magi doing duty
to the higher self
in a birthing place
for the Word Made Flesh
sharing our humanity's

subtly sublime unanimity's
enveloping luminosity's
clothing us in light
as we dare to reveal
a propensity for believing
answering
the unanswerable question,
keeping safe
the Heart's Disclosure.

Self-portrait

From canvas, uplifted eyes
blink a-moment's sunlight
as unwashed glass tries
my vision, lit-yellow a band
of dancing dust motes.

I put down the brush…

time's etching rush
scores face/form lines in youth,
storming memories that
cannot lie, mask or ask
too much of brush and paint
though no saint am I
brush-fletching arrows
striking their colours.

Windows are mirrors
reflecting sun-vistaed grasses
trees, flowers, shadowed/
unshadowed skies vaster
than shores, sea-wide horizons
where comparisons
are pointless, and age's lines
are only truth, thoughtfully
in my studio's hush, sooth,
forever.

Raindrop World

A rain shower's waterdrop
suspended into stillness
becomes
cosmic unto itself, a world
cloud towering
lightning struck apart
dowering
a manifested fullness

an 'Invitation to the Dance'
freeing
storms whirled
by divine splendour
in tempest charged thunder
impelling visions unfurled
violent incisions
of light-speared brightness
seeing
a mirroring lightening
far-out whitening
enhanced, evanescing
irradiation.

Ecce Homo 4 – Eyes on the Eternal

Forever, refusing withdrawn
gazes from the eternal
severing minds and senses
when infernal darkness
hazes hope, clear storming
the cyclic equinoctial gates,
they are a miracle
of non-conforming.

'I am the door,
the Initiator who rates as
guardian of the threshing floor
upholding St Theresa
above the spurious defences
of materiality.

'I am clear lenses
removing the blindness
of spiritual cataracts,
one who interacts
between time and eternity.'

Constable

The Water Mill

Far and near worlds
merge day's lapses
into sun-sinking evening's
leavening seasons
transitioning
as on the first day
by a river slipping easily
past bordering reeds.

The carter and his horse
ford slow-glinting water
clopping leisurely hooves
half smothered by flows
over mill wheels lapping
past trees on the bank
clustering
and brick-mellow cottages
green girdled as if
outgrowing earth-life
unspoiled by modernity
captured, painted
timed vision into memory
in passing.

Nocturne 5 – Hunted

Homing,
soft night-stolen running
over millennia of leaf litter
fearing Diana
stunning hope with her hunting
hound-stars swarming
night-timed
darker than a gloaming
releasing
their alarming footsteps
menacing
in cool black air
a bitter mockery of hope
fielding no sanctuary
from a merciless peering
admitting no bounds
to a searing blood lust
hunters
of the small and inconspicuous
haphazardly
under looming branches
spreading
beneath a hunter's moon
haunting home goers.

Cathedral in the Rain

Wandering
friendship's miles with me
recognising our leveller
tiling thoughts to see
a cathedral swept by rain
and on the road of pain
or long night watching
a cloud piercing spire
impaling a drooping sky
do not tire, try
awareness with a spur
of insight as I self-stir
to paint grey stones
washed clean over the bones
of centuries, cold, heat,
storm, and unpredictability.

Hope's ability
conquering holds friends
to a road cloud/misted
and a rain-cloaked hill
goal, goad, and beyond
the tyranny of distance
harmonic in convergence
with a lamp-lit evening.

A Strong Light

Day-clear ripple spreading light
strong, unmatched
by flaunting meridian power
when Avalon far away
hides apple blossom rings white
alone matched
by a phosphorescent shower
scattering radiance to stay
the heart's peace

when release
water/sun dancing a dawn song
glowing, shorn
of illusion is a bird's flight
becoming insight reborn
in sanctuary depths bright
beyond hearing and sight
'signs of the times' that
before a high-lit morning
cease to be.

Ecce Homo 5 – The Scourge

Scourging no detraction
from dignity is
curtains back-drawn
on outer world exposure
of establishment inaction
against indignity
and the scourged back torn
banners unfurling
for courage's action
against authority
half-born yet outrageously
challenging stones twirling
since time began, a cry:

*'Agnus Dei
qui tollis peccata Mundi,
miserere nobis…*

Ecce Homo!'

Turner

Sunset From a Train

Ah, the mastery of light
fire-wide skies ink-darkened
inside-out cloud patches
wind-speed whipped smoke
iron rumbling on iron
the wind bumbling
sunset racing towards night

passion trying
to capture the fury
latches on a need
creating image-wild stroke/
strikes through windows
opening
inhibition tumbling
endows a never-like-that seen
sunset on rough canvas
brush-whip coloured
watching a train approaching
freed from the choke
of passing moments
glory unbridled, painted
weathered endlessness.

Nocturne 6 – Dark Visions

Furniture looming shapes
black
mind cut-outs into visions
across night-spaced breathing
formlessly
imaginably are suggestive
but harmless?

Fear hovering gapes
across emptiness, a pack
of presences, incisions
into awareness seething
mindless
until touch, investigative
becomes a hold
making the darkness visible
and space no longer cold
filled with the invisible…

a becoming light.

Castle Loom in Dawn Light

Dawn light and mist
feather soft/gossamer thin
haze the loom
of morning turrets
in moments sun-rising
for a fortress
a residence
a shimmer twisted
pink-fine filtering, kin
to a hazed womb
of substance
from the sun emerging.

Moat water glimmering
a silver/white blaze
strengthening
as the veil, lifting
a turret's loom solidifying
stone grey
above water-light flashing
pallid into gold
is a tale
in time told.

Lord of the Sun

Paint the visions
singing
from heart-stopping dark
spark change-ringing
stark
emerging divisions
insinuating collisions
in creation, flinging
surging elements, the mark
of victory, Sun Lord.

How, can mere paint hoard
life's forms, Krishna,
Arjuna's chariot driving storms
the ultimata of victory?

Ongoing history
calling for fixed norms
is a drawn sword
flashing, a weeping willow
sighing andante cantabile
a wave's rearing billow
at the risen sun
a play in static hush
less half begun.

Ecce Homo 6 – The Image

Muffled restlessness
powering trains through darkness
fellow/watches travellers fixate…

on an image?

Mindfulness and courage
entrained in motion
unsightly, twisted shadows
levellers facing a single visage
or listlessness ignoring brightly
fixed-gazing eyes, whiteners
to conscience where courage
is demanded
or wilfulness perhaps
driving us to the lightness
of febrile wanderers, lest we…

in 'One' ourselves see.

Van Gogh

Sunflower King

Gold-haloed magic
dark/warm sun-hearted
dancing on earth-scented breezes
sunflowers opening
tossing, prancing
into light
earth, air infusing fire and water
seize the moment
for the painter's brush,

a rallentando hush
un-shadowing stillness, parted
from timing
as true gold unfriezes
powers untiming
and sunlit graces illuminating
purity's white impact chiming
shares in eternity with you
brother…of creation's fraternity
a rhyming splendour
fanned into colour.

Nocturne 7 – The Morning Star

Botticelli's dream, shell born
from sun-dappled foam
night to dawn beckoning
within the dome enclosed
crystal spheres, timing
a reckoning peace
above and below
evening's darkening stage
or at the gates of morning

transcendent, scorning
the incarnating round
being is, and becoming
under a faintly greying rim
echoing time's unheard sound
emanating night's dark cope
resting within the scope
of morning's hymn
far from home, pure gold
aslant yet still
at heaven's slow lightening
increasing, brightening
day's path while I decrease.

Residual leaven will cease
recalling splendours past
as a new visionary
riding daunting thunder's
lightning/dancing clouds
sees Venus –
'Bright and Morning Star'

and lost dreams are
recaptured incandescent
enthused by evenings
darkening yet heralding
the dawn, while she
one star…is ascending.

Dancing in the Corn

A riotous wildness,
beige/yellow containment
of palely green-shadowed corn
almost corps-de-balletic,
a toss/turn formation dance
restrained
yet life exploding
a fullness sunlit
entrainment
of elemental dancers born
in sun/shadow/fire's
sympathetic magic,
mysteriously a lance
passionately retrained,

the secret coding
to a painter's discipline
when summer heated day
flourishes, a surprise
until evening supervenes
as Compline, night's last
memorial chanted ray
leans into the dark
and gold/green's faded mark
is tomorrow's promise.

Does the Iris Remember?

Far from artifice and ordering
red, gold, blue
flaunted to shame the sun
in splendour

no loam pampered
your true home, no garden
artificial bordering.

Recalling,
thunder storming untamed
across water-worlds of cloud
ripple-reflected light, wind
rain, lightning, wildness
sweeping marsh/reed beds
unnaming
a mist/shrouded gaming
mantled-white playing,

elemental trickery denying
mild lit days shedding gold
matching your wild blooms…

Do you remember?

Ecce Homo 7 – Those Eyes

You have His eyes, Vincent.

Was your consent
so terrible a reckoning,
light and fire
burning a beckoning
through smoke of desire
hands outstretched
blessing your sacrifice?

Did a Provençal dream's
sunflower dancing gold
and iris blue
suffice, stretching a mind
awake, etching true
warm/hearted focus
on a storied theme
love's scheme of beauty,
the locus of a pain
surprised by you,
Vincent?

Sydney Nolan

Ned Kelly – First-class Marksman

Behind a mask this marksman,
an open window onto
'numero uno', personally
instrumental
in staccato questioning
is no king's or queen's man
authority investigating
but a disruptive scan,
a show of force
divorced
from green/brown landscaped
broken bush scatterings
however small
unrescued
by cultural significance
…or not,
a consequential goal
a lost soul, task unfinished,
a show of impotence
a cry in the dark;

the mark of Cain?

Night Watch

Navigating a river-in-the-sky
for love speared
on the Southern Cross,
night watches black formed
half waiting immensities looming
a significance of shapes
long-shadowing silences
innocently aware of loss

and conscience's equation
live or die…dramas drape cold
against skin, Outback brooding
dreams illimitably intense.

Sparking gold tributaries try
to outshine pale glittering
stardust veils scoping a painter's
imagination envisioning
high-sloped bulks blackening

but not debating
ten Commandments in desert tents
or releasing on a quickening sigh
love nailed to the Southern Cross.

Ned Kelly – The Trial

I confront faceless faces
in ostentatious marble halls
and pseudo-ecclesiastical
woodwork-varnished courtrooms;

'The trumpet shall sound…!'

as I pray for graces
when the inevitable outcome calls
for war, defeat, a fantastical
Eureka!

'The dead shall be raised…!'

for victory's celebratory looms
weaving the Southern Cross
into spirit lighted glooms
equality's pledges
in-thought fledges
and pain's dream, caught
not taught, or erased
as the trapdoor opens…

'and we shall be…rearranged?'

Love – In Light and Shadow

Love's landscaped light
Centre/red/stark ruggedness
and cloud-shadow sweeps
over grandeur eroded
edging austere aridity
in desert sparse shrubs
and grasses, intense
though less complex
than day/night
height/depth tiredness
as faith vertiginous leaps
aware, uploaded
by light/shadow timelines
above and below, in love
while thinking back
when water is stillness, slack
in a valley cleft/shaded
and love interacts unfaded
by light sky-clear high-riding,
fearing not
we are knowing
as children of the widowed one
that all may be well
no passing bell,
just love consciously growing.

Ecce Homo 8 – At the Crossroads

Under cloud driving darkness
the cross
is the crossroads
dreamed black, lightning etched
across sharp-smoothed horizons
against 'the dogs of war'
and thunderous stress
four outstretched ways meeting

after lost spirit descent
and no help fetched
for Krishna sacrificed, no orisons
offered, for fidelity no store
no less
than dark-matter's wave deleting.

Who guards the gouged-out roads,
goads an earth disturbed
turning the sod,
counters Kali Yuga
with the Song of God?

Nicholas Roerich

Altai Dreaming

Snow and pine-clad slopes
heart-pulsed by hidden lakes
the road in a mantra
snakes between dawn breaks
firing sunset blood
and tantra verse-lit in tropes
imaging a resonating soul
on a tone-struck singing bowl

a breaking shell, the goal
of spirit into bursting suns
belying coolness, the toll
of air as light's transparency
constancy in fullness married
to the sensory and spiritual
by a bell song calling
when selfhood plunged
like a heart-stopped arrow
into its own awakening
today/tomorrow in-let
from dawn to evening
light flooded, opening
…a self discloses.

Dare to Dream

Called out, a light shaft
a soundless way
over depth-blue chasms
hilltop snow sloped, silent
night/day reverberations

the intentions
in embattled moments
life raft riding
unpredictable wave spasms
of divine discontent

and divine intent
echo pyramid peaks
true/sharp song haunted
yet, when the harp note
struck, suspended
highlights
horizons of revelation
along a now trodden way
neither night nor day
are what they seem
for those with 'ears to hear'
who dare-to-dream.

Messenger of the White Burkhan

Peaked ghostly immanence
under paled moon-rising
radiating sounding light
across the eminence of history
into the morning,
messages a messenger
at midnight or meridian sun
in Altai's pristine clarity
of truth unveiled
divine light in rightness
for love, a heart's mystique
outpointing
singing a forested glory
dawn lightening

and guardian fivefold
Khan and Shaman
prophetic horseman white
as told, sharp two-edged
a sword so true and faithful,
Lost Word
as in the beginning tried
forever gold
once hidden on the way
be now…
upon the breath, open!

Road to the Seventh Gate

The road
is an ankle-turning roughness
a goad,
pain too sharp for less than love
as eyes rest on blue/green
from above seen
out of a shadowed cleft.

Will, the sky echo gold when
I, outsold am bereft
seeing only in the eyes of a dove
a hope that all is not vain?

Flying over green slopes
and forests singing blue
passing
from darkness to light
washed white
whiter than snow in the morning,

may love be the seventh gate,
opening…?

www.ingramcontent.com/pod-product-compliance
Lightning Source LLC
Chambersburg PA
CBHW062150100526
44589CB00014B/1776